ALL-PRO
BASEBALL STARS
1977

BRUCE WEBER

SCHOLASTIC BOOK SERVICES
New York Toronto London Auckland Sydney Tokyo

To Herman,
who taught me everything I know

The author wishes to express his thanks to the American and National League public relations offices, as well as to the major-league team publicists for their help in assembling the material for this book.

NOTE: Material for the All-Star profiles and the team previews went to press on December 17, 1976. For later developments through January 17, 1977, see the "Late News" on page 108.

Cover photo of Mark Fidrych by Dorothy Affa/Focus on Sports.

12 11 10 9 8 7 6 5 4 3   7 8 9/7 0 1 2/8

Printed in the U.S.A.   06

Contents

National League All-Stars 1976 1

American League All-Stars 1976 25

Major League All-Rookie Team 1976 49

National League Previews 70

American League Previews 83

Statistics 98

Predictions 107

Late News 108

Joe Morgan, the National League's Most Valuable Player

National League
All-Stars
1976

1B: Steve Garvey
2B: Joe Morgan
SS: Dave Concepcion
3B: Bill Madlock
OF: Garry Maddox
OF: George Foster
OF: Ken Griffey
C: Bob Boone
RHP: J.R. Richard
LHP: Randy Jones
RP: Rawly Eastwick

First Base
STEVE GARVEY
Los Angeles Dodgers

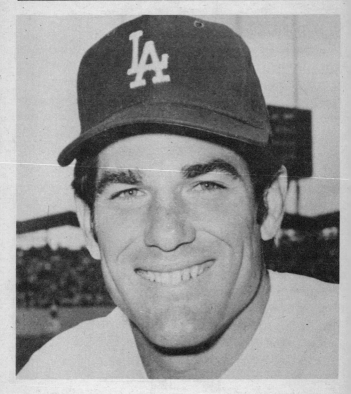

Steve Garvey's magic number is "200." It stands for 200 hits. It's Steve's goal—every year. He stencils it onto his batting glove.

He made it last year. Barely. Coming into September, he had 157 hits. His chances looked grim. But with 43 hits in the Dodgers' last 32 games, he did it. Right on the head—200!

It was something special. L. A.'s 28-year-old first sacker became the first Dodger ever to get 200 hits or more three years in a row. That includes the Brooklyn Dodgers as well as the Los Angeles Dodgers. And that takes in some of the game's greatest hitters.

Congratulations, Steve. But what made it so tough in '76? "I just wasn't getting the same number of good pitches," he says. "I walked more than ever."

That's true. Garvey drew 50 walks last year, 17 more than in 1975 and 19 more than in '74.

Despite the extra free passes, the 1974 National League MVP still snuck in his 200 hits and batted .317. That's his fourth straight year over .300.

Durable? That's Garvey. He and Pete Rose were the only National Leaguers to play in all 162 games in '76. Steve has missed only eight games in the last three seasons.

The 5-10, 190-pounder has some goals for '77, of course. "To start with," he says, "200 hits. I want to play in every game again. And I want 100 RBIs" (up 20 from last year).

What else? "I want to help the club win."

Second Base
JOE MORGAN
Cincinnati Reds

All-star second baseman? It's a joke. No one is close to Joe Morgan. The 5-7, 160-pound Morgan is a powerhouse. He's a little Red machine. He's also the No. 1 player in the game today.

By the time the 1977 World Series rolls around, Joe will be 34. That's no problem. "Joe gets better with age," says his manager, Sparky Anderson.

Morgan is baseball's one-man offense. You figure run production by adding runs scored plus runs batted in. Then you subtract homers (that would be a credit in both departments). Morgan's 1976 total? *Only* 197 runs. He had 111 "ribbies" (runs-batted in) and 113 runs scored (along with a career-high 27 homers).

"Think what his totals would be if he didn't miss 21 games with injuries," says manager Anderson. Hard to believe, Sparky. The rest of Joe's numbers: .320 batting average, 151 hits, 30 doubles, and five triples. And don't forget his 60 stolen bases.

What's Morgan's goal? "To be a perfect player," says little Joe. Some experts think he's there already. He helps himself by using a home videotape machine to study himself (and others) in action.

Other than that, Joe likes to forget baseball off the field. "I read and listen to music," he says. "I relax all day. Then, when I get to the park at night, I'm ready, really ready."

When the season ends, Morgan turns to tennis and golf. If he goes after those two sports like he goes after baseball, Jimmy Conners and Jack Nicklaus better watch out.

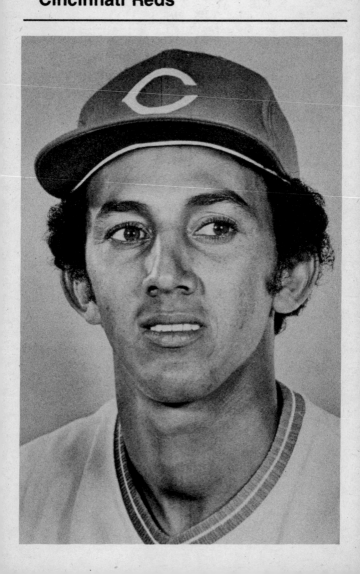

When we picked Larry Bowa as NL All-Pro shortstop last year, we got letters from all of Dave Concepcion's fans. (Dave, your friends write up a storm.)

Save your stamps, Concepcion-ites. Dave was the NL's No. 1 shortstop in 1976. And there's no reason to believe he won't repeat in 1977.

Concepcion's sure-handed fielding makes a big difference for the Big Red Machine. Playing on the Riverfront Stadium carpet, you need a steady shortstop. And no one is steadier than Dave.

Concepcion is 6-2 and weighs 175 pounds. That spells "Lean and Mean." He's like a vacuum in the field. He won another Golden Glove for his 1976 work.

But that's not all. Dave has become a hitter. His .281 average in 1976 tied his best full-season mark. He has come a long way since the .205 and .209 averages of 1971 and 1972.

The problem with a .281 average on the Reds is that everyone else hits even better. (The team batting average last year was .280, easily the majors' best.) But there are few shortstops who hit .281, and none who can do so many other things as well.

Dave is from Venezuela. That South American country turns out lots of good shortstops. The best, before Concepcion, was former All-Pro Luis Aparicio. Stand aside, Luis. Davey is No. 1 now.

Third Base
BILL MADLOCK
Chicago Cubs

    If you saw it in the movies, you wouldn't believe it. With one game remaining last season, Bill Madlock of the Cubs was hitting .333. Not bad. But it was only good for

8

second best in the National League. When you're the defending batting champ, second isn't good enough.

Ken Griffey of Cincinnati had a .338 average. A five-point lead. What could the 26-year-old Cub do?

Well, for starters, he could go four-for-four in the finale. Meanwhile Griffey batted—and failed—twice. Final marks: Madlock .339, Griffey .336.

The dramatic turn-around raised Bill's lifetime mark to a sparkling .337 (for three seasons) and gave him a second straight bat crown. He's the first Cub to do that since Cap Anson—remember him?—did it in 1887 and 1888. (No wonder you forgot!)

Though his average slipped from the .354 of 1975, overall 1976 was Madlock's best year in the majors. He played in more games (142), hit more doubles (36), and smashed more homers (15) for more total bases (257) for his highest slugging percentage (.500). He had more steals (15), walked more (55), and struck out less (27). Quite a year.

The 5-11, 180-pounder is equally proud of his year in the field. Once he was known as Stone Fingers at third base. No more. He cut his errors by one-third last season.

Madlock also had a club-high 12 game-winning hits (of the improved Cubs' 75 wins). Can he win the bat title again? The answer in Chicago: "Why not?"

Outfield
GARRY MADDOX
Philadelphia Phillies

Phillie fans weren't delighted when general manager Paul Owens sent Willie Montanez to the Giants for Garry Maddox on May 4, 1975. Willie is doing a fine job (in Atlanta now). But Garry is winning games—and division titles—in Phillie .

Maddox did everything the fans dreamed he could do last year. He hit, he ran, he fielded. And he did all of it very well, thank you.

Hitting? Maddox wore out National League pitchers. His .330 average was his best ever. And it was good for third in the NL behind Bill Madlock and Ken Griffey. The year included 175 hits, 37 doubles (tied for third in the league), six homers, and 68 RBIs. He also had six game-winning hits.

Running? Maddox stole 29 bases, eighth in the league and second on the club (behind Larry Bowa).

Fielding? He got his hands on everything hit in the middle of the Vet Stadium outfield. And those hands were steady. He made only six errors all season.

Maddox has a dream. It's to repeat as NL East champions and defeat Cincinnati in the playoffs. It would be a perfect end to a perfect season. Beating the hometown team and all. Garry, you see, was born in Cincinnati, 27 years ago.

If the 6-3, 175-pounder has another season like last year, the dream might just come true.

Outfield
GEORGE FOSTER
Cincinnati Reds

Opposing pitchers hate George Foster.
It's not just that he hits the ball hard (.306

average). Or that he hits it over buildings (29 big homers). Or that he hits with men on base (league-leading 121 RBIs).

That's part of it. But they also hate the fact that he steps out of the batter's box after every pitch. And they don't like the way he flips his big black bat around while he gets ready to hit.

Cincinnati fans, on the other hand, love it. They love everything George does. He's the power behind the Big Red Machine.

Every time the San Francisco Giants see Foster in left field for the Reds, they kick themselves. He belonged to them—until 1971. The Reds got him for practically nothing. And, though it took time, the trade has proven a steal.

George is 6-1 and weighs 190 pounds. Hard to believe, his waist size is only 30 inches. All his power is above the waist. He has a great upper body and a pair of unbelievably powerful arms. His favorite exercise is squeezing rubber balls. They give him the arm strength.

"My secret," says the 28-year-old, "is a quick bat. I'm not as strong as Johnny Bench or Dave Kingman. They can muscle the ball out of the park. I've got to make a solid hit with a quick bat."

The other Foster secrets? Clean living (he won't even drink coffee) and karate. "It helps my reflexes," says Foster.

Outfield
KEN GRIFFEY
Cincinnati Reds

Ken Griffey hails from Donora, Pennsylvania. No wonder he can hit. Thirty-five years ago, Donora turned out another "fair" hitter—Stan Musial!

The folks in Donora never realized that Griffey would become another super batter. He was a star in football and track. In fact, he was a *29th round* draft choice for the Reds. "We figured that with his ability to run and throw, he could become a player," says Cincy scouting boss Joe Bowen. And he has!

A great minor-league hitter, Griffey's bat went cold when he hit the majors in 1974. In fact, the Reds sent him back to Indianapolis to brush up on his hitting.

Then, in '75, it was the big leagues to stay. As a regular, he batted .305, racking up 38 infield hits along the way. What speed!

In '76, he was nothing short of super. A .336 batting average and 34 stolen bases. The powerfully-built 5-11, 200-pounder was one of the main cogs in the Big Red Machine.

What's in store for '77? "We're going to get Ken running more," says manager Sparky Anderson. "He could steal even more bases. And we'll get him to stretch more singles into doubles. With his speed, he should get 15 more doubles than he did last year."

That's a tall order. Griffey had 28 doubles among his 189 hits last year. But with his speed anything is possible. Forty-three doubles? Why not?

BOB BOONE

Philadelphia Phillies

It's tough to beat out Johnny Bench for anything. Especially for the spot as the National League's All-Pro catcher. But Bob Boone did it in '76.

16

It's kind of amazing, too. Just the year before Bob couldn't beat out Johnny Oates for the starting position on his own team!

But '76 was Bob's year. That's one of the reasons that '76 was the Phils' year, too. Boone, son of former major leaguer Ray Boone, put it all together. He had his best season at bat—and his best season behind the bat. All at once.

Though Bob was drafted as a third baseman (his father's position), the Phils made him a catcher in the Instructional League. It took a few years, but their gamble—and Bob's—paid off.

When Philadelphia stormed ahead of the NL East in June, Bob was right at the top of the parade. A Boone grand-slam homer won a big game. Then, two days later, he laid down a perfect suicide squeeze bunt to win another contest. In all, Bob had nine game-winning hits. Only Mike Schmidt, among the Phils, had more.

Though he batted only 361 times (in 121 games), Bob had 98 hits and 54 RBIs. He also drew 45 walks.

Defensively, Bob made only six errors and threw out dozens of enemy runners. His "cool" behind the plate helped calm many of the Phils' young pitchers.

If the Phils manage to win again, give much of the credit to their steady, young catcher.

Right-Handed Pitcher
J. R. RICHARD
Houston Astros

He's 6-8. He weighs 220 pounds. He plays
his home games at the Houston Astrodome.

And he doesn't play for the Houston Oilers of the NFL.

It's—who else?—J. R. (for James Rodney) Richard. On the mound, he's a monster. (Off the mound, too, for that matter.) When he unwinds that 6-8 frame and strides to the plate, look out. It seems he can almost hand the ball to the catcher.

Not really. But the big guy's fastball arrives in a hurry. Quickly enough to win 20 games for the 1976 Astros. No Houston pitcher has ever won more.

Richard has finally become a solid pitcher. He kept the Astros waiting long enough. In five previous NL seasons, he won only 23 games. He always knew how to strike out people. Problem was he walked too many.

It still bothers him at times. He struck out 214 in 1976 while walking 151. The difference was clutch pitching. When the chips were down, J. R. got 'em out. His ERA—a lifetime 4.37 coming into last season—dropped to 2.75.

A five-game winning streak from April 12 to May 7 was the Astros' longest last year. And his 13 strikeouts on closing day vs. San Francisco was also an Astro best. (J. R. shares the major league record for most strikeouts in a first start—15.)

J. R. swings a pretty mean bat, too. He swatted two homers last year. Believe it or not, only five Astros hit more.

Left-Handed Pitcher
RANDY JONES
San Diego Padres

Randy Jones went through two seasons last year. During the first half of 1976, he was the best pitcher in baseball. The second half? It was another story. Still, his 22-14 record and 2.74 ERA with a so-so Padre club was good enough to win him the NL Cy Young Award.

Jerry Koosman's fans argued bitterly. But the record clearly shows why Jones won the award. The 6-0, 180-pound slow-baller led the National League in wins (22), innings (315⅓), and complete games (25—in 40 starts). He was second in shut-outs with five and walked only 50 batters (nine intentionally).

At All-Star time last July, Randy was 16-3. He was the starter (and winner) for the National League in the classic. By July 28 his record had soared to 18-4. Randy (and his fans) dreamed about 30 wins.

It wasn't to be. He lost 10 of his last 14. The Padres didn't hit; Randy couldn't win. In those final 14 decisions, San Diego got him less than three runs per game. He had a 3.14 ERA over that period; it wasn't good enough.

The season wasn't all happy for Jones. There was an auto accident that knocked him out for a week in August and an injury that required an operation after the season.

"The doctor warned me I might never pitch again," says Jones. "Thank goodness it wasn't that serious."

Relief Pitcher
RAWLY EASTWICK
Cincinnati Reds

They call Sparky Anderson "Captain Hook." It has nothing to do with the character in Peter Pan. It's just that he'll take out one of his Reds' starting pitchers at the drop of a curveball. He gives 'em the hook.

It's not surprising. If you had someone like Rawly Eastwick ready in your bullpen, you'd just as soon have him in there, too.

With a name like Rawlins Jackson Eastwick III, you'd think he'd be playing polo somewhere. Names don't mean a thing. Rawly considers himself "The King of the Hill." He really believes it.

He's a good-sized king at 6-3 and 180 pounds. In 1975, as a rookie, his record was 5-3. But his 22 saves tied for best in the NL (with Cardinal ace Al Hrabosky). No one came close to Rawly in '76. He had 26 saves, seven better than Ken Forsch (Houston) and Skip Lockwood (N.Y.). His earned run average was a sparkling 2.08.

How does he do it? With his fastball. "He just fires it," says manager Anderson. "He says to the batter, 'here it is, try and hit it.' "

Rawly's biggest fan is catcher Johnny Bench. "He just keeps getting better and better," says the Reds' backstop.

Would Rawly like to be a starter? "I'd like to have a crack at it," he says. But it won't be soon. Not if Sparky Anderson can help it.

"Rawly's just too valuable in relief," says the Cincy skipper.

Thurman Munson, the American League's Most Valuable Player

American League
All-Stars
1976

1B: Chris Chambliss

2B: Bobby Grich

SS: Toby Harrah

3B: George Brett

OF: Mickey Rivers

OF: Ron LeFlore

OF: Reggie Jackson

C: Thurman Munson

RHP: Jim Palmer

LHP: Frank Tanana

RP: Bill Campbell

First Base
CHRIS CHAMBLISS
New York Yankees

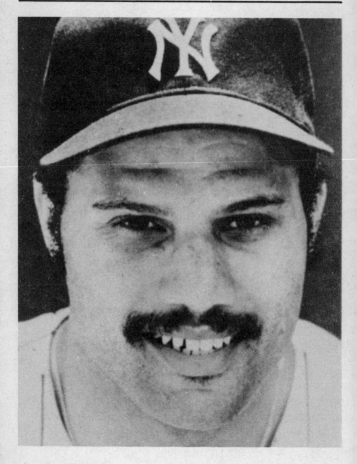

It was the biggest home run in New York
since Bobby Thomson's in 1951. Thomson's

"shot heard 'round the world" won the '51 NL pennant for the New York Giants. Chris Chambliss's last-of-the-ninth blast in the final game of the '76 playoffs gave the Yanks their first AL title since 1964.

It's the kind of thing 28-year-old Chris has been doing since he arrived in New York from Cleveland in 1974. He was part of a deal which saw the Yanks ship half their pitching staff to the Indians. The fans howled. They don't anymore.

Big (6-1, 209 pounds) Chris had a simply awful first season in the Big Apple. He hit .243 in 110 Yankee games. But that's behind him now. He's the man the New Yorkers most like to see at the plate when the chips are down.

Check these numbers: .293 average, 32 doubles, six triples, 17 homers, 96 RBIs, and a .441 slugging mark. All that and a pennant-winning homer. Quite a year!

Chambliss's performance makes him think he has finally found a home in New York. That's important to him. His dad was a Navy chaplain. The Chambliss family was always on the go.

Chris thought he would be in Cleveland forever. He was shocked when he was dealt to the Yankees. That may explain his poor '74 season. Now he's the big man at a big spot—first base for the Yankees. It has been an important position ever since Lou Gehrig held it for 15 seasons.

Second Base
BOBBY GRICH
California Angels

Gene Autry got rich as a movie cowboy. He chased outlaws all over the early West. Now and then he stopped to sing a song. But like all the good guys, he always got his man.

Gene is a little older now. And a lot heavier. But as owner of the Cal Angels, he still always gets his man.

Like Bobby Grich. The Orioles' four-time Golden Glove second-sacker was one of the prize catches of the free agent draft. And cowboy Gene got him.

A one-time minor league player-of-the-year, Grich is a steady hitter. Nothing great. His .266 in '76 was his second best average ever, and five points over his lifetime mark. But he led the Orioles in runs scored (93) and doubles (31). And he cracked 13 homers and knocked in 54 runs. Okay.

The rangy 6-2, 180-pounder really shines in the field. He combines great range, a strong arm, and a sturdy body. He failed to lead American League second basemen in chances for the first time in years last season. But only because of an early season injury that kept him out of the lineup for about two weeks.

Now Grich is going home. He grew up in Long Beach, California, and still lives there. That's only 30 minutes from Anaheim Stadium. But he's going home to a strange position. Angel manager Norm Sherry plans to use Bobby at shortstop. He hasn't played there since his minor league days.

Can Bobby make the switch? The word around the league is: "You can bet on it!" With Grich's talent, he may be the 1977 American League All-Star *shortstop!*

Shortstop
TOBY HARRAH
Texas Rangers

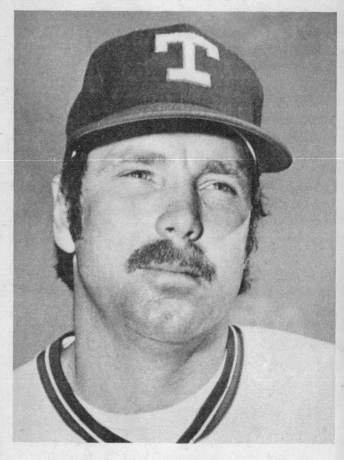

Over the winter, Ranger manager Frank
Lucchesi planned to make Toby Harrah his

third baseman in '77. Similar plans have been made before. And every year Harrah ends up as the All-Star shortstop.

This time may be different. Lucchesi made the 28-year-old Harrah his third baseman five games before the end of last season. It was his first game there in nearly two years. Lucchesi says Toby is at third to stay.

Why the move? Some critics say Harrah can't cover enough ground at short. But they've always been saying that. The Rangers always had someone ready to push Toby out. First it was Jim Mason, now with Toronto. Then Pete Mackanin, who hangs his hat in Montreal. And then Roy Smalley—now at Minnesota.

This time, however, the new man at short is Bert Campaneris. The Rangers signed the A's free agent in November. But even at third base, Toby won't hurt them.

He was the team's leading hitter in '76, though his .260 average was 23 points off his best-ever '75 record. Part of the problem was a severely sprained ankle which hurt him all season—in the field, on the bases, and, says Harrah, at bat.

Still he chipped in with 15 homers and 67 RBIs. Not many Rangers did better (Toby was third on the club in both areas).

"I'm ready to move to third," says the 6-0, 180-pounder. "If Frank wants me there, I'll be there."

Third Base
GEORGE BRETT
Kansas City Royals

George Brett may be the AL's All-Pro third baseman. But around the Brett home, Charlie Lau is man of the year.

Lau? Sure. He's KC's batting coach. And

Brett, the AL's No. 1 hitter, gives Charlie the credit for *making* him a hitter.

Charlie must have done quite a job. A last at-bat inside-the-park homer gave George a .333 average and his first AL bat crown.

It was his second straight .300 year. George also led the league in hits (215) and triples (14) for the second straight year. In doubles, his total of 34 tied him for second behind teammate Amos Otis.

Of course, Charlie Lau doesn't swing the bat for George Brett. George has to do that. And Lau is his biggest fan.

"George is an artist at the plate," says Lau. "People don't appreciate that. He hits line drives all the time. And he hits them where he wants to. That's an artist."

Royal manager Whitey Herzog loves Brett, too. "He comes to play every day," says the boss. "Unless something is broken—and badly—he's out there." Right, Whitey. George played in 159 Royal games in '76, the same total as in '75. "George may be the best all-around player in the American League," insists Herzog.

Shortstop Fred Patek thinks Brett's greatest progress has come in the field. "He's really improved. It helps a shortstop when the third baseman cuts off the balls in the hole."

Watch Brett this season. He—and the Royals—can both make it two straight titles.

Outfield
MICKEY RIVERS
New York Yankees

In the winter of '76, Yankee fans cried over the loss of Bobby Bonds. "For Mickey Rivers?" they wailed. "What is he going to do?"

There was no crying during this winter of '77. They found out exactly what Mickey could do. Win them their first American League pennant in 12 years, that's what!

Rivers, who's 28, moves constantly. He wiggles. He jumps. Most of all, he excites. Enemy pitchers hate when Mickey gets on base. He did that 196 times last year (184 hits, 12 walks). Fifty times he tried to steal, and 43 times he made it. The man is lightning on the bases.

In leading the Yanks to that long-hoped-for pennant, Mickey hit .312. That was his best year ever in the majors. But people were waiting for that. He hit .300 or better in all five minor league seasons.

Mickey kills the opponents on defense, too. With his great speed, he catches balls that no other centerfielder could reach. Considering the size of centerfield at Yankee Stadium, that's a big plus. If Mickey has a weakness, it's his arm. But he gets his throws off so quickly, he makes up for the lack of a great arm.

The Yanks drew 2,012,434 fans to their beautiful new ballyard in the Bronx last year. Mickey made all of them happy. But no one was happier than his new teammate, Thurman Munson. The Yankee catcher says, "I'm glad he's on my side. You just can't throw him out stealing. If he gets a good jump, forget it."

Outfield
RON LeFLORE
Detroit Tigers

"The Ron LeFlore Story." It's beautiful!
What a story! Hollywood will love it.

Four years ago, Ron LeFlore was in jail. He never played high school baseball. The Tigers spotted his raw skill in prison games. They took a chance and signed him.

After 134 minor league games, LeFlore came home—to Detroit. He may never leave.

In 1975, Ron established himself as a big-leaguer. He enjoyed a pretty fair season. A .258 average, eight homers, 37 RBIs. Okay.

Suddenly, 1976. A super year for the soon-to-be 25-year-old. He hit .316, got 172 hits, knocked in 39 runs, scored 93—despite missing the last three weeks with a knee injury.

Not bad for a guy who didn't start on opening day. Didn't even get a chance until April 17. Ron didn't blow it.

The 6-0, 200-pounder smashed a double in his first at bat. He hit safely the next day...and the next. Fact is, the opponents didn't stop him until May 28. In between, he hit safely in 30 straight games, longest in the majors in six years, longest in the American League in 30, and longest in Detroit in 42 seasons.

Talk about speed. Ron has it. Blinding speed. He stole 58 bases, second only to Oakland's Billy North. It was more than any Tiger since Ty Cobb in 1916.

The Tigers may be ready to go places. And Ron LeFlore will lead them.

Outfield
REGGIE JACKSON
New York Yankees

Need a loan? Call Reggie Jackson. He's loaded. He's got plenty of Yankee owner George Steinbrenner's money. Between $2 million and $3 million—probably closer to the three. According to the contract it'll be arriving in hunks until about 1996. Color Reggie green—as in money.

Green or otherwise, Reginald Martinez Jackson is one of baseball's most colorful players. "I didn't come to New York to become a star," he said when he signed with the Yanks. "I brought my star with me."

That's true. The solidly-built 6-0, 205-pounder has been a star since his first full season with Oakland in 1968. He smashed 29 homers and banged in 74 runs that season. And except for one downer—1970—it has been star-time ever since.

Reg is a great talker. He loves the swinging life. (That was one big plus for New York.) Last spring, when Oakland traded him to the Orioles, he quit baseball. "I can only play on the West Coast," he said. A raise—to $140,000—coaxed him out of retirement.

He gave the Orioles 134 great games—27 homers, 91 ribbies, a .277 average, fine defense, a super throwing arm.

But despite the raise, Reg never signed a 1976 contract. That made him a free man at season's end. The numbers were scary—three million, four million. But Steinbrenner had what Jackson wanted—money and New York.

"If I played in New York," Reg used to say, "they'd name a candy bar after me." He's there now. Candy makers, please take note.

Catcher
THURMAN MUNSON
New York Yankees

The Yankees have always had great catchers. Bill Dickey and Yogi Berra are in the Hall of Fame. Elston Howard was super. Thurman Munson is right up there with them.

He has two straight .300 years, including .302 last year. He has two straight 100 RBI years, including 105 ribbies in 1976. He's tough (152 games in 1976). And he's a great team leader.

When the going gets tough, Munson is at his best. The Yanks would rather forget the World Series. You hate to remember a 4-0 blowout. But don't blame Thurman.

He had nine hits in 17 at-bats. That's a .529 average. The Yanks had eight runs in four games. Thurm, the league MVP, knocked in two of them. He handled 28 chances without an error. Sure, the Reds stole seven bases. But they stole them on the Yankee pitchers, not Munson.

New York isn't surprised at Munson's success. The Yanks drafted him No. 1 out of Kent State in 1968. After 99 minor league games, he hit the big time. He was AL Rookie of the Year in 1970, after hitting .302.

If Munson has a weakness, it's his throwing style. He whips the ball sidearm, to save time on his throws to second. But he makes up for it with his smarts. Yankee pitchers call him "The Brain." They love to see #15 behind the batter when they work.

Right-Handed Pitcher
JIM PALMER
Baltimore Orioles

It's getting to be a habit. American League Cy Young Award winner: Jim Palmer. He owns three of those beautiful trophies. No other American Leaguer can make that claim.

Jim would love to have ex-Red Sox manager Darrell Johnson with him when he gets the award. It was Johnson who left Palmer off the American League's 1976 All-Star Team. "I wasn't at my best during the first half of '76," says Palmer, "but I was as good as some of the guys Johnson picked."

By the end of the season, there was no question. Jim ended up as the league's top winner (22) and posted a 2.51 ERA.

That's a routine performance for the Birds' 6-3, 196-pounder. He has the best winning percentage among active pitchers (.652). His overall earned run average is 2.61, one of the best of all time.

It wasn't always that way. Despite a fast start (he was the youngest pitcher ever to toss a World Series shutout), Palmer struggled through the early years. When the Kansas City and Seattle (now Milwaukee) teams joined the AL in 1969, Palmer was available in the expansion draft. They passed him up.

Good thing for Baltimore. In 1969, Jim went 16-4, then racked up the first of seven 20-win seasons in 1970. Only a poor 1974—Jim had a bad elbow—stopped his string of super seasons.

At age 31, Palmer should be at his peak. He still has the great fastball—and he's as smart as any pitcher around.

Left-Handed Pitcher
FRANK TANANA
California Angels

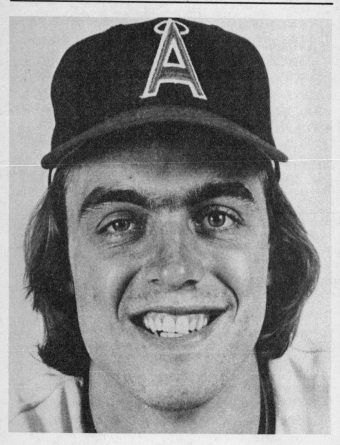

Angel fans are spoiled. They expect good pitching. When Frank Tanana takes the mound, they usually get it. Now if they only got a little hitting to go with it.... But that's another story.

At age 23, Frank Daryl Tanana is one of baseball's best pitchers. His 19 wins (against 11 losses) set a major league high for the fastballer. His 2.43 earned run average was third best in the league. He struck out 261, second only to teammate Nolan Ryan. And his complete game stats—23 in 34 starts—were tremendous.

When you realize that the Angels' season record was 76-86 and the team batting average was a puny .235, Tanana's numbers are downright amazing.

How does fame effect the 6-3, 195-pound Tanana? He loves it. "I love people," he says. "The fans are great. I don't mind signing autographs. I love talking to the fans."

The fans love Frank, too. With his record, it's no wonder. But even more important, the opponents respect him. Says Boston catcher Carlton Fisk: "He can throw hard, but his curve puts you in the dirt while the ump calls strike three."

Frank added a pair of shutouts to his previous total of 10. But one of his best '76 performances was a sparkling 2-1 win over Vida Blue and the A's last August 6. Winning the tough ones is what Tanana does best.

Frank's goal? He's not modest. "I want to be the greatest pitcher of all time." He's already one of the best around.

Relief Pitcher
BILL CAMPBELL
Boston Red Sox

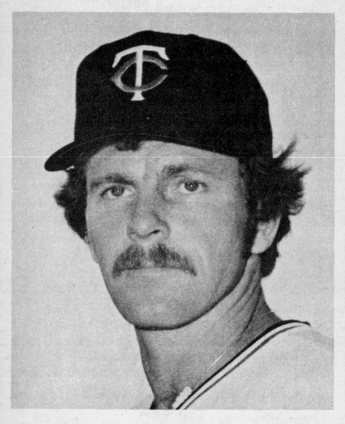

Bill Campbell took a chance. After Bill's so-so '75 season, the Minnesota Twins' owner Cal Griffith offered him $30,000 for '76. Not enough, said Campbell.

Bill gambled by playing out his option. The gamble paid off beautifully. Whatta season! He was the AL's best reliever. He won 17 games (lost only five) and saved 20 more. His ERA was 3.00 for 167 2/3 innings—a record for American League relievers.

The result? Bill was one of the most sought-after free agents. Just a couple of days after the re-entry draft, he signed with the Red Sox. The deal? It's reported to be for *one million dollars* over four years. Quite an improvement over the $30,000 he got from Minnesota.

Campbell is happy. But the folks he left behind aren't. "I don't know where we'd have been last year without Bill," says Twins' manager Gene Mauch. He means it. Campbell took his strong right arm into 78 Twins' games. His total of wins and saves (37) accounted for nearly half of the club's 85 victories.

The 28-year-old Campbell was a starter until he joined Minnesota at mid-1973. He quickly turned to relief work, training himself to get ready with only a dozen warm-up pitches. That's far different than the 15-minute pre-game warm-up that starters receive.

In the spring of '76, the gamble was Campbell's. He delivered. Now the Red Sox are gambling that he's for real. Don't bet against it!

Mark "The Bird" Fidrych, Rookie of the Year

Major League
All-Rookie Team
1976

1B: Jason Thompson
2B: Willie Randolph
SS: Garry Templeton
3B: Ron Jackson
OF: Tom Poquette
OF: Larry Herndon
OF: Ellis Valentine
 C: Butch Wynegar
 P: Mark Fidrych
RP: Butch Metzger

First Base
JASON THOMPSON
Detroit Tigers

Jason Thompson could have picked a better time to splash onto the major league scene. Unfortunately he came up with the Tigers at the same time as Mark "The Bird" Fidrych. The fans hardly knew Jason was alive. But the Tiger opponents did.

Thompson smashed 17 homers for Detroit last year. That's the most for any Tiger rookie since Rudy York, one of baseball's greatest sluggers, boomed 35—in 1937. Though he hit only .218 and his glovework is just okay, the home run threat makes him a valuable addition to the club.

Jason's overnight success leaves a trail of egg (scrambled, please) on the faces of baseball scouts. After his junior year in college (Cal State-Northridge), the Central Scouting Bureau didn't even file a report on him. The Tigers took a chance, picking him fourth on the 1975 free-agent draft.

He finished '75 in the minors (.324 in AA ball) and started there (at AAA Evansville, Ind.) in '76. But three weeks into the season, Detroit called for him. Good move, Tigers.

No one was more surprised at Jason's instant success than Thompson himself. "I really didn't play first base regularly until my last year in college," he says. "Then, after only 79 games in the minors, I'm a major-league first baseman. Wow!"

The Tigers still have problems. But thanks to Jason Thompson, first base isn't one of them.

Second Base
WILLIE RANDOLPH
New York Yankees

On Dec. 11, 1975, the Yankees sent one of their top pitchers, Doc Medich, to Pittsburgh. They picked up a couple of good vets—pitchers Ken Brett and Dock Ellis.

But the key man was a 21-year-old rookie, Willie Randolph.

The Yanks knew what they were doing. The 5-11, 160-pounder from Brooklyn pulled the Yankee infield together. The hometown boy gave them what they wanted—the best second-base playing at Yankee Stadium since Bobby Richardson of a dozen years ago. And he helped them win a pennant.

New York had seen Willie play second in a Yank-Pirate exhibition game before the '75 season. That's when they decided they needed him. They paid a lot for him. (Medich always did well in New York.) But Randolph was worth it.

The big question mark on Willie's back was his bat. Could he hit major-league pitching? Answer: Yes. He'll never lead the league. But his bat will never hurt the club.

He started the season like a house afire. The average: around .330 for the first month or so. He had to slow down—and he did. But his season mark of .267 was more than many expected. Despite missing 37 games with injuries, Willie had 115 hits (15 were doubles), 40 RBIs, and 37 stolen bases. Only Mickey Rivers, among the Yanks, had more steals.

Willie was super in the field, too. He made the double play and scooped up everything he could reach—and that was plenty.

The Yanks are set at second!

Shortstop
GARRY TEMPLETON
St. Louis Cardinals

The Cards fell out of the National League East race early last year. Some insist they were never in it. With the season shot, the Cards decided to try their young shortstop at Tulsa—Garry Templeton. He may be in St. Louis forever.

The Cardinals have a fine young infield. Garry may be just the guy to turn it into a championship infield.

He's 5-11 and 170 pounds. Good enough size for a shortstop. He has great range in the field—going right or left. And his arm? It's a rifle—an accurate one, too.

A switch-hitter, his batting has been suspect. Right-handed, he's fine. Lefty? He still needs some work. But Cardinal bosses are pleased with his progress from the left side.

His speed is tremendous. "He has to learn how to use it," says his Tulsa manager, Ken Boyer. "He has to learn how to play the hitters. And he must work on his hitting. But remember, this kid is only going into his third year of pro ball."

That's right. At age 20 last summer, Garry was the youngest player in the National League. He could be the Cards' shortstop for at least a decade and a half.

"With Templeton at short and (Mike) Tyson at second," says Cardinal ace Lou Brock, "you could see a lot of T 'n' T double plays around here."

Third Base
RON JACKSON
California Angels

Third base was probably the best position
among big-league rookies in '76. The Mets'

Roy Staiger, the Braves' Jerry Royster, the White Sox' Kevin Bell, the Cards' Hector Cruz.

But none of 'em did as well as the man from Disneyland. Jackson hit only .227 (none of the rookies did very well at the plate). But he showed a good arm, great range, and overall ability at the hot corner.

Even though he didn't hit for average, the 23-year-old from Birmingham, Alabama, did some great clutch hitting for the Angels.

Let's go back to the opener of a twin-bill against Kansas City last May 29. California trails 2-0 with two out and two on in the ninth. Up steps Jackson. A game-tying triple, followed by an Andy Etchebarren single (scoring Jackson) gives the Angels a 3-2 win. They go on to sweep the double-header.

Two weeks later, in Detroit, Ron goes 4-for-5 with a homer and double to key a 10-7 Cal win.

That's what the Angels are looking for from Jackson. When he's hot, he's hot. In his first major-league game (Sept. 12, 1975), he went 4-for-5 against Kansas City.

"He may have bad days," says manager Norm Sherry. "But he doesn't let them get him down. Ron is a super kid. He doesn't pop off. He's a hard worker. And he gets along beautifully with everyone."

Outfield
TOM POQUETTE
Kansas City Royals

In *Baseball Stars '76*, we told you that K.C. had only one rookie-to-watch: Tom Poquette. Thanks, Tom, for making us look good.

There's no question. Poquette was one of the keys to the Royals' AL West title. Despite a serious injury—fractured cheekbone, concussion—Tom played in 104 K.C. games and hit a sparkling .302. He trailed only AL bat leaders George Brett and Hal McRae for Royal honors.

A former football running back at Memorial High School in Eau Claire, Wis., Poquette has had injury problems throughout his career. The 25-year-old has had two knee operations. Both resulted from a baseball accident—he stepped in a drainage ditch.

The second operation, on Jan. 19, 1975, ruined Tom's 1975 season. He played about two-thirds of the year at Jacksonville, Fla. He hit .256 and had lost some speed. There were questions.

No more. Tom was super last year. In addition to the .302 average, Poquette had 104 hits, 30 of them for extra bases. He had 34 ribbies and six steals.

The 5-11, 175-pound left-handed hitter has only one problem. He hustles too much. Last season's injury came in a battle with the leftfield fence in Royals' Stadium. Tom lost.

"Poquie was great," says manager Whitey Herzog. "I love guys who hustle. We knew he could play defense. But his bat! That was great. He sparks the whole team."

Outfield
LARRY HERNDON
San Francisco Giants

The Giants' history is long and glorious. It dates back to the late 1800's in New York. They've always had great outfielders. With Larry Herndon, they may just' have another one.

Larry wanted to be a football player. He agreed to take a football scholarship from Tennessee A&I in 1971. Then came a change of mind. Selected third by St. Louis in the 1971 baseball draft, Herndon forgot football.

For awhile, it looked like he made a mistake. Larry's progress was a little slower than he dreamed it would be. In fact, until last May 1, the 6-3, 188-pounder was playing for the Giants' Phoenix farm club.

Then came his big break. Von Joshua went into a slump and manager Bill Rigney put the newcomer into the lineup in centerfield. Within a month, Larry had everyone buzzing. He hit like crazy—over .400 the first month. He caught every ball hit anywhere in his neighborhood. And he hustled like mad. The Giant fans, as few as there seem to be, loved every minute.

The .400 average was too good to last, of course. Larry slipped to .288, still the best Giant average. Despite hitting in the lead-off spot, he knocked in 23 runs. And his 12 stolen bases tied Gary Matthews and Bobby Murcer for the club lead.

Offense or defense, Larry does it all. Football's loss is surely the Giants' gain!

Outfield
ELLIS VALENTINE
Montreal Expos

Every day is Valentine's Day in
Montreal. That's the first thing new man-

ager Dick Williams will learn. Take out your lineup card and write down: "Valentine, centerfield." Then worry about the other eight spots.

That's what former manager Karl Kuehl did after bringing Ellis up from the Expos' Denver farm club last July 16. Montreal just seemed to play a little better with the lanky 6-4, 205-pounder in the outfield.

The big right-hander, who'll be 23 around All-Star time this year, was born in Arkansas. But he grew up in baseball-mad Los Angeles. "I've always thrown things," he says. "Bottles, rocks, whatever was there. I guess that's why I throw so well."

He's great at catching the ball, too. Expo pitcher Woodie Fryman marvels at his ability in the field. "He gets them in the gaps and he catches those bloopers. You can't imagine what that does for a pitcher's confidence."

Ellis also knows what to do with a bat in his hand. His .279 batting average was more than the Expos expected. He also had 15 doubles, seven homers, and 39 RBIs in just 94 games, most of them batting in the lead-off spot. Add to that 14 stolen bases, and you have an explosive threat.

Montreal had the worst team in the majors in '76. No question about it. But they played just a little better with Ellis in the lineup. The future looks great!

Catcher
BUTCH WYNEGAR
Minnesota Twins

The big noise out of Minnesota last season—that was Mr. Harold Delano

Wynegar, Jr., better known as Butch. The Twins' rookie star looks like he'll be the backstop in Bloomington for the next ump-teen seasons.

The story of the 21-year-old is nothing short of fantastic. He spent the 1975 season at Reno in the California League. That's Class A. It wasn't bad for a start. A .314 average, 19 homers, 112 ribbies. But Class A to major leagues? You'd better believe it.

Butch was in the Twins' lineup on open-ing day and he stayed right there. Why not? In that first game, he knocked in Minneso-ta's only run in a 2-1 loss. A week later, he homered off Catfish Hunter to give the Twins a 5-4 win.

That was just the start. The youngster with the super arm (he fires nothing but strikes to second base) hit more than .300 for the first half of the season. He made the American League All-Star team and, when he pinch-hit (a walk), became the youngest ever to play in the classic game.

The switch-hitting Wynegar slumped over the second half of the season. The long hours behind the plate tired him out. Still he finished with a fine .260 average (.268 lefty and .244 righty). Add 10 homers (eight of them lefty) and 69 RBIs and you have quite a year.

"My rookie year was like a dream come true," says Butch. "Simply sensational." The Twins hope for many more.

Starting Pitcher
MARK FIDRYCH
Detroit Tigers

When was the last time a rookie was the most talked-about player in baseball? We can't remember, either.

Mark Fidrych is in a class by himself. Who else stands in front of 55,000 people talking to a baseball? Only The Bird.

"C'mon," he says to the ball. "Gotta keep

it down. Let it fly." And, more often than not, the ball did exactly what Mark wanted it to do.

The Fidrych story is a little unbelievable. He wasn't on the Tigers' spring '76 roster. He didn't make his first start until May 1.

Then it happened. Start followed start. Win followed win. In a national TV game, Mark wiped out the Yanks, 5-1, to raise his record to 8-1. The 51,000-plus fans wouldn't leave until Mark came back to the field. He did. They screamed. He blew kisses. He was famous.

The 6-3, 175-pound Fidrych made baseball's club-owners rich. He made 29 starts and drew 901,239 fans. That's an average of 31,077 (and lots of cash in the till). At home—even better. In Fidrych's 19 Tiger Stadium starts, Detroit drew 605,677 fans (31,878 average per game). Not a bad draw. Mark's 1976 salary—the minimum $16,000!

He'll do a lot better in '77. But money doesn't seem to mean much to the 23-year-old. "If I wasn't here," he says, "I'd be somewhere else pumping gas."

Forget the gas, Mark. The man who talks to balls led the majors in ERA (2.34) and the AL in complete games (24) on the way to a 19-9 season and American League Rookie-of-the-Year honors. Only the second rookie ever to start an All-Star game, Mark won't be pumping gas for awhile.

Relief Pitcher
BUTCH METZGER
San Diego Padres

    For all those casual fans who think
Randy Jones is the Padres' only pitcher,
think again. Big Butch Metzger is one of
the best young relievers in baseball.

That's a real shocker. Throughout most of a six-year minor league career, Butch was a starter. Even in 1975, at Hawaii, he started 20 times in his 36 appearances. That's all over now. The 6-1, 185-pounder figures to be the big man in the Padre bullpen for a long time.

Last year he racked up an 11-4 mark (he was 10-0 in late August). His 77 appearances set a record for the Padres—and for all major league rookies! His 10 straight wins also set a club record (Randy Jones had the old mark of seven) and his 16 saves tied the club CAREER record.

The 24-year-old, once a San Francisco Giant, made a living in '76 with only three pitches—a fastball, curve, and change-up. "Butch is unreal," says manager John McNamara. "He throws high fastballs—and gets away with them." Why? "The ball rises. Some of them rise out of the strike zone—and still the batters swing."

Metzger blames his late-season slump on overwork. "I was dead tired. Nothing else. They wanted me to rest—afraid I'd hurt my arm—but I didn't want to. I wanted to help the club."

That's understandable. The Padres didn't have much in the bullpen department. Metzger had 16 saves. The rest of the San Diego relievers had only two between them.

National League

1976 Standings

WEST

	Won	Loss	Pct.	GB
Cincinnati	102	60	.630	—
Los Angeles	92	70	.568	10
Houston	80	82	.494	22
San Francisco	74	88	.457	28
San Diego	73	89	.451	29
Atlanta	70	92	.432	32

EAST

	Won	Loss	Pct.	GB
Philadelphia	101	61	.623	—
Pittsburgh	92	70	.568	9
New York	86	76	.531	15
Chicago	75	87	.463	26
St. Louis	72	90	.444	29
Montreal	55	107	.339	46

and Previews for 1977

CINCINNATI REDS
NL West

Pete Rose

The world champs have no weaknesses. None. They have baseball's best infield, a super outfield, underrated pitching, a great catcher, a fine manager. The best NL team ever? Maybe.

They'll miss Tony Perez's bat (.260, 91 RBIs) and Don Gullett's arm (11-3, 3.00 ERA). But there are replacements.

Joe Morgan (.320, 27 homers, 111 ribbies) is the game's No. 1 player. He does it all. Dave Concepcion (.281) is the best fielding shortstop — and he had 15 game-winning hits last year. Pete Rose (.323) keeps killing people. Dan Driessen (.247 as a part-timer) will replace Perez.

The outfield of George Foster (.306), Cesar Geronimo (.307), and Ken Griffey (.336) is the best there is. Catcher Johnny Bench usually is, too, though he suffered at bat (.234) last year.

The pitchers are young. But they're proven winners. There's nothing wrong with Fred Norman (12-7), Pat Zachry (14-7), Gary Nolan (15-9), and company. And Rawly Eastwick (11-5) may be baseball's best reliever.

Rookies to watch: P Larry Payne, P Tom Hume, 1B Dave Revering.

LOS ANGELES DODGERS
NL West

Doug Rau

After 23 years under Walter Alston, the Dodgers enter '77 with a new field boss — long-time coach Tom Lasorda. He has only one problem — the Cincinnati Reds. They happen to play in the same division.

The Dodgers are pretty good. Their 92-70 mark last year was excellent. But not in the same league with Cincinnati.

L. A. has some fine players. All-pro 1B Steve Garvey (200 hits, .317 average) may be the best. But speedy Dave Lopes (.241, 63 steals) is fine at second. So are SS Bill Russell (.274) and 3B Ron Cey (.277).

The Dodgers spent the off-season looking for outfield help. But they'll be better off if Dusty Baker (a slumping .242) can bounce back. Reggie Smith (.253, but .280 with L. A.) is a proven pro.

Pitching is a strength, with Doug Rau (16-12), Rick Rhoden (12-3), and Don Sutton (21-10) all fine. Charlie Hough (12-8, 2.20 ERA, 77 games) needs help in the bullpen.

Rookies to watch: P Dennis Lewallyn, C Kevin Pasley, OF Glenn Burke, OF Joe Simpson.

HOUSTON ASTROS
NL West

Cesar Cedeno

The '76 Astros finished 80-82. It was the fifth best record in the club's 15-year history. And it was good for a solid third in the NL West.

Astros bosses must have been happy. They kept the same cast through the winter trading period.

Houston made only one deal. They sent veteran outfielder Greg Gross (.286) to the Cubs for someone named Julio Cesar Gonzalez. Houston fans can't understand it.

Fortunately, Houston has plenty of outfielders, led by Cesar Cedeno (.297), Leon Roberts (.289), and Jose Cruz (.303). The Astros felt they could spare Gross for a speedy young infielder (Gonzalez).

Manager Bill Virdon has a fine young pitching staff. Ace righty J. R. Richard (20-15) was only Houston's second 20-game winner. Ken Forsch was tops in the bullpen before an injury put him out of action. Houston pitchers tossed 17 shutouts (second best in the NL) on the way to 42 complete games and a 3.56 team ERA.

Rookies to watch: OF-1B Jim Fuller, OF Bob Detherage, P Joe Cannon.

SAN FRANCISCO GIANTS
NL West

John Montefusco

Giant field boss Joe Altobelli is one of six new managers in the NL. He could be in the tightest spot. While the Giants' NL West rivals have improved, San Francisco has gone backwards.

The Giants were grim (74-88) last year. They lost power-hitting Gary Matthews (.279, 84 RBIs) in the free-agent draft. They failed to sign any free agents themselves.

They made two big deals — both with St. Louis. The new Giants are outfielders Willie Crawford and Vic Harris and pitchers John Curtis and Lynn McGlothen. The deals rate a toss-up.

Crawford is a key. The 30-year-old joins youngster Larry Herndon (.288) and vet Bobby Murcer (.259) in the Giant outfield. They're okay.

The infield is punchless. And the pitchers aren't much — except for Jim Barr (15-12) and outspoken John "Count" Montefusco (16-14). The bullpen is strong with Dave Heaverlo (4-4), Randy Moffitt (6-6), and Gary Lavelle (10-6).

Last place? A possibility.

Rookies to watch: P Greg Minton, P Bob Knepper, P Frank Riccelli, P Terry Cornutt, P Monroe Greenfield, IF Johnnie LeMaster, C Gary Alexander, OF Jack Clark.

SAN DIEGO PADRES
NL West

Mike Ivie

The Padres are for real. Really! They've always had pretty good pitching. Now, for the first time, they have a little hitting to go with it.

Make that a lot of hitting. No. 1 addition was Oakland catcher Gene Tenace (.249). Then they picked up slugger (25 homers) George Hendrick from Cleveland. Add to that ace reliever Rollie Fingers, another of the A's free agents, and you have a real pennant threat. Padre fans have suffered through eight long years waiting for this one.

The returnees are solid. There's Cy Young Award pitcher Randy Jones (22-14). He must bounce back from an October arm operation. Last year's rookie star Butch Metzger (11-4) should combine with Fingers to give San Diego a great bullpen.

Dave Winfield (.283, 69 runs-batted-in) joins Hendrick and speedy Jerry Turner (.267) in the outfield. Vets Mike Ivie (.291) and Doug Rader (.257) anchor the infield. But youngsters at second and short may hurt the Padre pennant run.

Rookies to watch: SS Bill Almon, 2B Mike Champion, LF Gene Richards, P Dave Wehrmeister, P Mike Dupree.

ATLANTA BRAVES
NL West

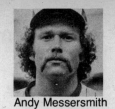
Andy Messersmith

The Braves used 45 players in a 70-92 1976 season. The '77 Braves would prefer using fewer.

Their first step was sending five players and $200,000 cash to Texas for slugger Jeff Burroughs. Atlanta Stadium is made for sluggers. Welcome, Jeff.

They spent even more money — about $1.3 million — for free-agent Gary Matthews. Gary and Jeff would give Atlanta a great outfield. But commissioner Bowie Kuhn spent the winter checking the signing of Matthews.

There's talent elsewhere. Nifty 1B Willie Montanez can handle a bat (.321 for Atlanta after coming from the Giants) and glove. SS Darrel Chaney (.252) must reduce his errors.

Atlanta's catching is ordinary, with Biff Pocoroba (.241) and Vic Correll (.225). Rookie Dale Murphy (.267 at Savannah) could help.

Phil Niekro keeps winning (17-11), even at age 38. Andy Messersmith should improve on his 11-11 mark. His ERA was a decent 3.04. Mike Marshall (6-3) is the top reliever.

Rookies to watch: P Rick Camp, C Dale Murphy, IF Pat Rockett, OF Brian Asselstine, OF Alvin Moore, OF Barry Bonnell.

PHILADELPHIA PHILLIES
NL East

Mike Schmidt

Last September, when the Phils nearly blew a 15-game lead, manager Danny Ozark was in trouble. Phillie hung on, of course, and now Danny has a new two-year contract. And maybe another pennant or two.

The Phils lost second-baseman Dave Cash (.284) to Montreal in the free-agent draft. But they picked up a new first baseman in the Pirates' Richie Hebner, a .277 lifetime hitter.

The rest of the cast is just about the same. 3B Mike Schmidt (.262) is the NL homer (38) and strikeout (149) champ. He had 17 game-winning hits in '76. With 1B Dick Allen (.268) gone, Phillie power must come from LF Greg Luzinski (.304, 21 HRs). Larry Bowa (.248) is solid at short, as is all-pro catcher Bob Boone (.271). Terry Harmon (.295) could replace Cash at second.

Pitching, led by lefty Steve Carlton (20-7) is in good hands. Larry Christenson (13-8), Tom Underwood (10-5), Jim Lonborg (18-10), and Gold-Glover Jim Kaat (12-14) are the starters. Gene Garber (9-3) and Tug McGraw (7-6, 2.50 ERA) run the bullpen.

Rookies to watch: P Randy Lerch, OF Rick Bosetti, 2B Fred Andrews.

PITTSBURGH PIRATES
NL East

Dave Parker

The Bucs had a 92-70 record last year. So they made few changes. Right? Wrong. There'll be plenty of new faces at Three Rivers Stadium in '77.

First is manager Chuck Tanner. Pittsburgh sent catcher Manny Sanguillen (.290) and a bunch of cash to Oakland for their new field boss.

The Pirates made their bullpen stronger by adding lefty Grant Jackson (7-1) and righty Rich Gossage (9-17 as a White Sox starter). They also got lefty Terry Forster, once the Al's top fireman, from Chicago. Dave Giusti (5-4), Kent Tekulve (5-3), and Larry Demory (10-7) return to the Buc bullpen. Jerry Reuss (14-9), John Candelaria (16-7 with a no-hitter), Bruce Kison (14-9), and Jim Rooker (15-8) are the best starters.

Power? The Bucs have plenty — with Dave Parker (.313), Al Oliver (.323), and Bill Robinson (.303). That's some outfield. Though he's 36 years old, Willie Stargell (.257) can still hurt the opponents.

Rookies to watch: OF Omar Moreno, OF Tony Armas, OF Miguel Dilone, P Doug Bair.

NEW YORK METS
NL East

Jerry Koosman

Pitching, they say, is 80 percent of baseball. The Mets have great pitching. The other 20 percent makes them just another ball club.

Lefty Jerry Koosman (21-10) had his best year ever last year. Though No. 1 pitcher Tom Seaver slipped to 14-11, his 2.59 ERA was third best in the NL. And southpaw Jon Matlack (17-10, 2.95 ERA) was super too. Reliever Skip Lockwood (10-7, 19 saves) was the find of the year. Yes sir, the Mets have the arms.

The other eight positions give them problems. Outfielder-first baseman Dave Kingman provides power. He hit 37 homers, second best in the NL, despite missing 39 games with a broken hand. Injury-prone John Milner (.271, 15 homers) delivers in the clutch. Aging Joe Torre hit .306, but played full-time in only 79 games.

If catcher Jerry Grote (.272), a great glove man, retires, young John Stearns moves up to No. 1.

The Mets get decent infielding from 3B Roy Staiger, SS Bud Harrelson (when he's healthy), and solid pro 2B Felix Millan (.282).

Rookies to watch: OF Lee Mazilli, P Jackson Todd, IF Randy Trapp, P Dennis Solari.

CHICAGO CUBS

NL East

Jose Cardenal

The last time the Cubs were in a pennant race, Leo Durocher was the manager. Now Leo's old buddy Herman Franks is the field boss. But they won't be in the pennant chase.

The Cubs' talent is thin. There's Rick Monday at first. He had a super '76 with 32 homers, 77 ribbies, and a .272 average. Jose Cardenal, at age 33, is coming off a great season — .299 and 23 stolen bases. CF Jerry Morales hit .274 and had 12 game-winning hits. So did 3B Bill Madlock whose .339 average led the NL for the second straight year. That's about it.

With not much to trade, the Cubs didn't do much trading. They picked up spray-hitting Greg Gross from Houston and so-so outfielder Jim Dwyer from the Mets.

So-so is the word for Cub pitching. Only Ray Burris (15-13 with four shutouts) and Rick Reuschel (14-12) were winners for the 75-87 ballclub. The bullpen crew features rookie ace Bruce Sutter (6-3) and Paul Reuschel (4-2), Rick's brother.

Rookies to watch: P Mike Krukow, P Donnie Moore, P Willie Prall, OF Ed Putman, 1B Jerry Tabb, OF Jim Tyrone.

ST. LOUIS CARDINALS
NL East

Lou Brock

New manager Vern Rapp's Cards stayed out of the free-agent market last winter. But the trading market? The Cards were plenty busy.

Key pickups include former Card Ken Reitz (back from San Francisco), a solid third-sacker; pitchers Larry Dierker and John D'Aquisto; and minor-league MVP outfielder Roger Freed.

The fine young infield returns, including first-sacker Keith Hernandez (.289), second baseman Mike Tyson (.286), and shortstop Garry Templeton (.291). Along with Reitz, they could be the Busch Stadium infield for 10 years.

Centerfielder Bake McBride (.335) must bounce back from knee surgery last August. Lou Brock (.301) is still super despite his age (36).

The Cards are deep in starting pitchers, led by Bob Forsch (8-10), John Denny (11-9), Pete Falcone (12-16), and D'Aquisto. Solid catcher Ted Simmons (.291) is the hurlers' best friend.

New faces: P Mike Caldwell, 3B Dave Rader, P Steve Dunning, IF Pat Scanlon, OF Tony Scott.

Rookies to watch: None.

MONTREAL EXPOS
NL East

Dave Cash

The most improved team in the NL East? Probably. But no one needed improvement like the Expos. Their 55-107 record was easily their worst since their expansion season of 1969.

What do you do? First, hire manager Dick Williams, a pennant winner at Boston and Oakland. Then sign Phillie free-agent 2B Dave Cash (.284). Shore up your infield with slugging Cincinnati first-baseman Tony Perez. Deal for ex-Cardinals Bill Grief, Angel Torres, and Sammy Mejias.

Next, the rebuilding project. Only a few positions are set. Perez and Cash join catcher-outfielder Gary Carter (.219) and rookie-flash Ellis Valentine (.279, 14 straight stolen bases). SS Tim Foli (.264), OF Del Unser (.228), and pinch-hitter Jose Morales (.316) are solid pros.

Pitching may be thin, because starter Woodie Fryman (13-13) and busy reliever Dale Murray (4-9) went to Cincinnati in the Perez deal. Steve Rogers, who missed a month last season, was 7-17 but deserved better. Righty Don Stanhouse was okay (9-12).

Rookies to watch: P Bill Atkinson, P Gerald Hannahs, P Joe Keener, P Larry Landreth, IF Rodney Scott, OF Warren Cromartie, OF Andre Dawson, OF Gary Roenicke.

American League

1976 Standings

WEST

	Won	Loss	Pct.	GB
Kansas City	90	72	.556	—
Oakland	87	74	.540	2½
Minnesota	85	77	.525	5
California	76	86	.469	14
Texas	76	86	.469	14
Chicago	64	97	.398	25½

EAST

	Won	Loss	Pct.	GB
New York	97	62	.610	—
Baltimore	88	74	.543	10½
Boston	83	79	.512	15½
Cleveland	81	78	.509	16
Detroit	74	87	.460	24
Milwaukee	66	95	.410	32

and Previews for 1977

KANSAS CITY ROYALS
AL West

Amos Otis

Can the Royals hold off California? Will they win their second straight AL West title? Those are the big questions facing KC this year.

KC features the AL's top two hitters of '76 — All-Pro 3B George Brett, (.333) and the AL's best designated hitter Hal McRae (.332). Slugging first-sacker John Mayberry (.232) bounced back from a slow start to hit 13 homers and knock in 95 runs. Tiny SS Fred Patek (.241) stole 51 bases. That infield is super.

Famous Amos Otis (.279, 40 doubles) is the outfield key. His playoff injury surely cost KC in the championship series. Rookie star Tom Poquette hit .302 despite crippling injuries.

Ex-Brewer Darrell Porter joins Buck Martinez (.228) in the fight for the catching spot. Another Milwaukee export, Jim Colborn (9-15), enters the pitching derby with righties Dennis Leonard (17-10), Doug Bird (12-10), and Marty Pattin (8-14) and lefties Larry Gura (4-0) and Paul Splittorff (11-8). Mark Littell (16 saves) leads the bullpen crew.

Rookies to watch: IF U. L. Washington, OF Willie Wilson.

OAKLAND ATHLETICS
AL West

Vida Blue

The Unknown Soldiers: That's the 1977 Oakland A's. Charles O. Finley lost just about everything from his 1972-74 world champs. Gone are Joe Rudi, Bert Campaneris, Sal Bando, Gene Tenace, and Rollie Fingers, along with Don Baylor, obtained from Baltimore for Reggie Jackson last year. Three more A's — pitchers Glenn Abbot and Leon Hooten and outfield Gary Woods — went in the expansion draft.

What's left? Not much. New manager Jack McKeon has young Phil Garner (.261) at second base. Speedy Claudell Washington (.257) and solid Bill North (.276) anchor the outfield. Aging Ron Fairly (.239) could be the first baseman. Manny Sanguillen (.290), who came from Pittsburgh for manager Chuck Tanner, will catch and do the designated hitting.

All-star lefty Vida Blue (18-13, 2.35 ERA) is easily the best pitcher. The rest are so-so, including Stan Bahnsen (8-7), Dick Bosman (4-2), Jim Todd (7-8), and Mike Torrez (16-12).

Youngsters like OF Denny Walling (.257 at Chattanooga) and C Jeff Newman (.268 at Tucson) must come through.

Rookies to watch: SS Rob Picciolo, OF Mark Williams, P Chris Batton, P Rick Tronerud.

MINNESOTA TWINS
AL West

Lyman Bostock

Owner Cal Griffith said that the Twins wouldn't go crazy over free agents. They didn't. And they came up empty.

Too bad. The Twins, 76-83 in 1975, turned things around (85-77) in '76. Now the move toward the top may come to a grinding halt.

The Twins' off-season losses were heavy. All-star reliever Bill Campbell (17-5) went where the money was — to Boston and $1 million. Pitcher Bill Singer and outfielder Steve Braun were among the expansion losses.

Meanwhile, back in the Twin Cities, 1B Rod Carew, five-time AL bat king, comes off a non-winning .331 season. Not bad. Other big sticks: outfielder Lyman Bostock (.323) and rookie catching star Butch Wynegar (.260).

Right-fielder Larry Hisle (.272) might be Gene Mauch's lead-off man. Danny Ford (.267), Mike Cubbage (.257), and Steve Brye (.264) are okay. Pitching, led by Dave Goltz (14-14), is the Twins' weakest point.

Rookies to watch: P Jim Gideon, IF Randy Bass, OF Bob Gorinski, OF Willie Norwood.

CALIFORNIA ANGELS
AL West

Bobby Bonds

Angel owner Gene Autry made free agents Don Baylor, Joe Rudi, and Bobby Grich very happy last winter.

The new Angels made the California fans very happy, too. They bought an Angel record total of season tickets.

If the new players can win a pennant, they'll make Autry very happy. A complete circle.

Ex-A's Baylor (.247) and Rudi (.270) and former Oriole Grich (.266) give Cal a solid attack and super defense. The Angels already had great pitching.

Ah, yes. The pitching. It warms the heart of manager Norm Sherry, a former big-league catcher. There's lefty Frank Tanana (19-10), the AL's best. And smoke-thrower Nolan Ryan (17 wins, seven shutouts). And second-year righty Paul Hartzell (7-4). And hard-luck Gary Ross (8-16, but a 3.00 ERA). Great!

Grich, if he can make the switch to shortstop, and second baseman Jerry Remy (.263) make Cal solid up the middle. Catcher Terry Humphrey (.245) is a fine glove-man. Oft-injured Bobby Bonds (.265) can make the outfield great.

Rookies to watch: P Mike Overy, C Danny Goodwin, 1B Willie Mays Aikens, OF Gil Flores.

TEXAS RANGERS
AL West

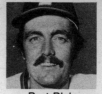
Bert Blyleven

They do things big in Texas. Like when they decide to trade their slugger. The Rangers sent 18-homer, 86 runs-batted-in man Jeff Burroughs to Atlanta. In return, they got five — count 'em, five — Braves. Some of them may help.

The new Rangers include outfielders Ken Henderson (.262) and Dave May (.215), and pitchers Carl Morton (4-9), Roger Moret (3-5), and Adrian Devine (5-6). If Morton can return to form, the Rangers will win the trade.

The biggest Texas winter pickup was shortstop Bert Campaneris (.256), a free agent from the A's. He'll move Toby Harrah (.260) to third base — or out of Texas altogether.

Bert Blyleven, despite a 13-16 record, is a solid pitcher. So is free-agent pickup Doyle Alexander (13-9). Mike Wallace was 3-2 at St. Louis in '76.

Underrated Tom Grieve (.255) is the outfield leader. He slammed a team-high 20 homers last year. The rest of the group, including Len Randle and Juan Beniquez, was ordinary.

Rookies to watch: P Bobby Cuellar, IF Bump Wills.

CHICAGO WHITE SOX
AL West

Jorge Orta

Sox owner Bill Veeck advertised for new players in the *Sporting News* last fall. He didn't get the big names he hoped for. But he did get a whole bunch of new faces.

One of them is manager Bob Lemon, a Hall of Fame pitcher. Lemon may have to do some pitching himself. The Sox sent nearly half of their '76 staff packing — including Pete Vuckovich, Rich Gossage, Terry Forster, and Jesse Jefferson.

But they picked up solid 3B Eric Solderholm (out all of '76) from Minnesota, C Dave Duncan from Baltimore, OF Richie Zisk from Pittsburgh, and P Steve Stone from the crosstown-rival Chicago Cubs.

The Sox needed new faces. Their 64-97 mark last year was enough to wreck Veeck. Outfielder Ralph Garr was the only .300 hitter (exactly .300) on the club. The team bat mark was .255.

Other "pros" included double-play experts Bucky Dent (.246), Jorge Orta (.274), catcher Brian Downing (.256), and rookie Chet Lemon (.246). Power comes from Jim Spencer (.253 and 14 homers).

Rookies to watch: P Chris Knapp, P Ken Kravec, P Larry Monroe.

SEATTLE MARINERS
AL West

Ruppert Jones

Mariner management loves its new team's chances. As much you can love an expansion team's chances.

Manager Darrell Johnson, ex-Red Sox boss, looks to his pitchers for quick help. Lefty Rick Jones was 5-3 for the '76 Red Sox. His ex-teammate Dick Pole, a right-hander, was 6-5 at Boston. Seattle also counts on rookie righty Gary Wheelock (15-8 at Salt Lake City).

Ex-Pirate Craig Reynolds, obtained for pitcher Grant Jackson, is ticketed for shortstop. Outfielder Steve Braun (.288, 61 RBIs at Minnesota) is a pro.

Another Mariner key is speed. "We have some real flyers," says manager Johnson. Outfielder Dave Collins stole 32 bags in 99 games with the '76 Angels.

Another flyer is Ruppert Jones, Seattle's No. 1 draft choice. He hit .262 with 19 homers and 16 steals at Omaha.

Rookies to watch: P Gary Wheelock, If Jose Baez, OF Ruppert Jones, OF Carlos Lopez.

NEW YORK YANKEES
AL East

Graig Nettles

George Steinbrenner, who builds ships, makes lots of money. George Steinbrenner, who owns the Yanks, is spending all of it.

The Yanks won it all in the AL last year. Then they lost the World Series. Steinbrenner spent a zillion bucks over the winter seeing that it won't happen again.

All-pro Reggie Jackson ($3 million) might be the man. He gives the Yanks power — and a great arm in the outfield which had none. Cincinnati's 11-3 left-hander Don Gullet ($2 million) joins a pitching staff of Catfish Hunter (17-15), Dock Ellis (17-8), Ed Figueroa (19-10) and Ken Holtzman (14-11). Wow!

The Yanks are loaded everywhere. There's all-pro catcher and AL MVP Thurman Munson (.302), clutch-hitting first-sacker Chris Chambliss (.293, 96 RBIs), AL homer-king Graig Nettles (.254, 32 HRs, 93 ribbies), speedy CF Mickey Rivers (.312), and solid Roy White (.286).

If the Yanks are weak anywhere — and that's a big *if* — it's at shortstop.

Rookies to watch: P Ken Clay, SS Mickey Klutts, OF Kerry Dineen, OF Terry Whitfield.

BALTIMORE ORIOLES
AL East

Mark Belanger

For a decade and a half, the O's have been the AL's biggest winners. Forget it. They're down — and maybe out.

The free-agent draft just about killed them. Reggie Jackson (.277, 27 homers) went to the Yanks. All-star second-baseman Bobby Grich (.266) is no Angel to Baltimore fans. Pitcher Wayne Garland (20-7, 2.68 ERA) left for points west (Cleveland).

What's left? Vet SS Mark Belanger (.270), coming off his best season. Slugging OF Ken Singleton (.278), with 13 homers and 70 ribbies. Young 3B Doug DeCinces (.234), one of the most sought-after Orioles during the winter.

Cy Young winner Jim Palmer (22-13, 2.51 ERA) is the kingpin of the mound staff. Palmer is unhappy over the O's prospects. Lefty Rudy May (15-10) returns as does ace reliever Tippy Martinez (5-1).

The key to the Oriole future is youth. Like lefty 1B Eddie Murray. But he probably cannot beat out vet Lee May (.258, 109 ribbies). OF Andres Mora, a 21-year-old prospect, may be a year away.

Rookies to watch: 2B Rich Dauer, SS Kiko Garcia.

BOSTON RED SOX
AL East

Luis Tiant

Like Humpty Dumpty, the Sox had a great fall last summer. The 1975 AL champs could do no right all season.

All the king's horses and men couldn't help old Mr. Dumpty. But manager Don Zimmer, starting his first full season, thinks he can do better in Boston.

Carl Yastrzemski, now 37, was the Sox MVP last year, with a .267 average and 102 RBIs. Second-year man Fred Lynn (.314) must bounce back from a 10-homer, 65-ribbie season. Same for Jim Rice (.282).

Slugger George Scott, back from Milwaukee, should help in a big way. Another Brewer returnee, outfielder Bernie Carbo, is a plus. Rick Burleson (.291) is a top-flight shortstop.

The AL's top reliever, Bill Campbell (17-5), is a free-agent pickup from Minnesota. He joins ageless Luis Tiant (21-12), Fergie Jenkins (12-11), Rick Wise (14-11), and Reggie Cleveland (10-9). Super Carlton Fisk (.255, a disappointment) is their catcher.

Rookies to watch: P Don Aase, P Bob Stanley.

CLEVELAND INDIANS
AL East

Jim Bibby

Cleveland pitchers should send up the most smoke signals in '77. The Indians spent $2.3 million to land ex-Oriole Wayne Garland for the next 10 years. He makes a strong pitching crew stronger.

Ex-Royal Al Fitzmorris (bought from Toronto) joins righties Dennis Eckersley (13-12), Pat Dobson (16-12), and Jim Bibby (13-7, 3.20 ERA) and lefty Rick Waits (7-9) to give Cleveland solid mound work.

But offense? That's another thing. First, Cleveland gave away its No. 1 hitter, Rico Carty, in the expansion draft. A mistake. But the Indians righted the wrong. They gave up catcher Rick Cerone and outfielder John Lowenstein to get their super designated hitter (.310) Carty back.

Unfortunately, the Indians also traded their top power man, outfielder George Hendrick, to San Diego. Hendrick hit 25 homers for the '76 Tribe. That was nearly one-third of the club total.

Ex-Angel Bill Melton may provide the power for the Indians, who are deep at shortstop and catcher, as well as in the outfield.

New faces: OF John Grubb, C Fred Kendall, IF Hector Torres, 1B Andre Thornton.

Rookies to watch: SS Alfredo Griffin, IF Dave Oliver, OF Vassie Gardner, P Tommy McGough.

DETROIT TIGERS
AL East

Rusty Staub

The 1976 Tigers were 16 games better than the '75 version. A similar improvement in '77 may win them a pennant. It isn't likely.

Chief surprise, of course, was right-handed pitcher, Mark "The Bird" Fidrych. Mr. All-Everything went 19-9 with 24 complete games and an unbelievable 2.34 ERA. John Hiller (12-8) is the Fidrych of the bullpen. The rest of the staff: ordinary, including Dave Roberts (16-17), Ray Bare (7-8), and Vern Ruhle (9-12).

Detroit got nothing in the free-agent scramble. They should have. The Tigers aren't deep. All-star Ron LeFlore (.316) is great. Outfield mate Ben Ogilvie (.285) might be. Plodding Rusty Staub in right can hit (.299, 96 RBIs).

Infielder Luis Alvarado (.280 at Tulsa, a St. Louis farm) joins rookie 1B star Jason Thompson (17 homers), SS Tom Veryzer (.234), and slick fielding 3B Aurelio Rodriquez (.240). Detroit needs help at second. Catchers Bruce Kimm (.263) and John Wockenfuss (.222) have retired Bill Freehan.

Rookies to watch: OF Dan Gonzales, OF Tim Corcoran, P Dave Rozema, P Bob Sykes, C Lance Parrish, 3B Phil Mankowski.

MILWAUKEE BREWERS
AL East

Sixto Lezcano

The Brewers had better get a maid. With all the housecleaning they did this off-season, they'll need one. After a 66-95 season, the changeover was a must.

A big plus is former Oakland 3B Sal Bando. He's a winner. Another new man is 1B Cecil Cooper who hit .278 for Boston in '76, including .400-plus against Milwaukee. (George Scott and Bernie Carbo go back to Boston.) A deal with Kansas City brought Jamie Quirk, who can play five positions, and OF Jim Wohlford.

Young (21) vet Robin Yount (.252) at short may be the only infield holdover. Cooper will be at first and Bando at third, with Tim Johnson (.275) possibly at second. Quirk, Wohlford, and Sixto Lezcano (.285, 56 RBIs) are the likely outfielders.

Righty Jim Slaton (14-15), lefties Bill Travers (15-16) and Jerry Augustine (9-12) head the mound staff.

Rookies to watch: P Gary Beare, P Barry Cort, P Sam Hinds, IF Jim Ganter, IF Lenn Sakata, OF Dan Thomas.

TORONTO BLUE JAYS
AL East

John Lowenstein

Jay owners spent $5.2 million for 30 players at the AL expansion draft. They were had. As usual, expansion produced a bunch of no-names for the new clubs.

Manager Roy Hartsfield and GM Peter Bavasi loaded up at baseball's two key spots — pitcher and catcher. For the mound staff they picked up Bill Singer and Ted Garvin (Twins), Pete Vuckovich (White Sox), Steve Hargan (Rangers), Dave Lemanczyk (Tigers), and Mike Willis (Orioles).

Toronto is even stronger behind the bat. They've got Alan Ashby (from Cleveland for pitcher Al Fitzmorris), Rick Cerone (also from the Indians), Ernie Whitt (Red Sox), and vet Phil Roof.

The deal that brought Cerone to Toronto also brought John Lowenstein, a power man with a puny .205 average. The pair cost the Jays .310 hitter Rico Carty. At 37, he didn't fit their plans.

There are few other names. It could be a long year in Canada.

STATISTICS
1976

NATIONAL LEAGUE

Individual Batting
(380 or more at-bats)

*Bats Lefthanded   #Switch Hitter

Player & Club	PCT	G	AB	R	H	HR	RBI	SB
Andrews, Robert, Hou. . . .	.256	109	410	42	105	0	23	7
Baker, Johnnie, L.A.	.242	112	384	36	93	4	39	2
Bench, Johnny, Cin.	.234	135	465	62	109	16	74	13
Bowa, Lawrence, Phil.# . .	.248	156	624	71	155	0	49	30
Brock, Louis, St.L.*	.301	133	498	73	150	4	67	56
Buckner, William, L.A.* . .	.301	154	642	76	193	7	60	28
Cabell, Enos, Hou.	.273	144	586	85	160	2	43	35
Cardenal, Jose, Chi.	.299	136	521	64	156	8	47	23
Cash, David, Phil.	.284	160	666	92	189	1	56	10
Cedeno, Cesar, Hou.	.297	150	575	89	171	18	83	58
Cey, Ronald, L.A.	.277	145	502	69	139	23	80	0
Chaney, Darrel, Atl.*	.252	153	496	42	125	1	50	5
Concepcion, David, Cin. . .	.281	152	576	74	162	9	69	21
Crawford, Willie, St.L.* . .	.304	120	392	49	119	9	50	2
Cruz, Hector, St. L.	.228	151	526	54	120	13	71	1
Cruz, Jose, Hou.*	.303	133	439	49	133	4	61	28
Davis, William, S.D.*	.268	141	493	61	132	5	46	14
Evans, Darrell, Atl.-S.F.* .	.205	136	396	53	81	11	46	9
Foli, Timothy, Mtl.	.264	149	546	41	144	6	54	6
Foster, George, Cin.	.306	144	562	86	172	29	121	17
Fuentes, Rigoberto, S.D.#	.263	135	520	48	137	2	36	5
Garrett, R. Wayne, N.Y.-Mtl.* . .	.231	139	428	51	99	6	37	9
Garvey, Steven, L.A.	.317	162	631	85	200	13	80	19
Geronimo, Cesar, Cin.* . .	.307	149	486	59	149	2	49	22
Gilbreath, Rodney, Atl. . . .	.251	116	383	57	96	1	32	7
Griffey, G. Kenneth, Cin.*	.336	148	562	111	189	6	74	34
Gross, Gregory, Hou.* . . .	.286	128	426	52	122	0	27	2
Grubb, John, S.D.*	.284	109	384	54	109	5	27	1
Hebner, Richard, Pitt.* . .	.249	132	434	60	108	8	51	1
Henderson, Kenneth, Atl.#	.262	133	435	52	114	13	61	5

Player & Club	PCT	G	AB	R	H	HR	RBI	SB
Ivie, Michael, S.D.	.291	140	405	51	118	7	70	6
Johnstone, John, Phil.* ..	.318	129	440	62	140	5	53	5
Kendall, Fred, S.D.	.246	146	456	30	112	2	39	1
Kessinger, Donald, St. L.#	.239	145	502	55	120	1	40	3
Kingman, David, N.Y.	.238	123	474	70	113	37	86	7
Kranepool, Edward, N.Y.*	.292	123	415	47	121	10	49	1
Lopes, David, L.A.	.241	117	427	72	103	4	20	63
Luzinski, Gregory, Phil. ..	.304	149	533	74	162	21	95	1
Mackanin, Peter, Mtl.	.224	114	380	36	85	8	33	6
Maddox, Garry, Phil......	.330	146	531	75	175	6	68	29
Madlock, Bill, Chi........	.339	142	514	68	174	15	84	15
Matthews, Gary, S.F.	.279	156	587	79	164	20	84	12
Metzger, Roger, Hou.# ..	.210	152	481	37	101	0	29	1
Millan, Felix, N.Y.	.282	139	531	55	150	1	35	2
Milner, John, N.Y.*	.271	127	443	56	120	15	78	0
Monday, Robert, Chi.* ...	.272	137	534	107	145	32	77	5
Montanez, Guillermo, S.F.-Atl.* ...	.317	163	650	74	206	11	84	2
Morales, Julio, Chi.......	.274	140	537	66	147	16	67	3
Morgan, Joe, Cin.*	.320	141	472	113	151	27	111	60
Mumphrey, Jerry, St. L.#	.258	112	384	51	99	1	26	22
Murcer, Bobby, S.F.*	.259	147	533	73	138	23	90	12
Oliver, Albert, Pitt.*	.323	121	443	62	143	12	61	6
Parker, David, Pitt.*	.313	138	537	82	168	13	90	19
Parrish, Larry, Mtl.	.232	154	543	65	126	11	61	2
Perez, Atanasio, Cin......	.260	139	527	77	137	19	91	10
Perez, Martin, Atl.-S.F.....	.257	124	428	49	110	3	32	3
Rader, Douglas, S.D.	.257	139	471	45	121	9	55	3
Reitz, Kenneth, S.F.	.267	155	577	40	154	5	66	5
Robinson, William, Pitt. ..	.303	122	393	55	119	21	64	2
Rose, Peter, Cin.#	.323	162	665	130	215	10	63	9
Royster, Jeron, Atl.......	.248	149	533	65	132	5	45	24
Russell, William, L.A.	.274	149	554	53	152	5	65	15
Sanguillen, Manuel, Pitt...	.290	114	389	52	113	2	36	2
Schmidt, Michael, Phil....	.262	160	584	112	153	38	107	14
Simmons, Ted, St.L.# ...	.291	150	546	60	159	5	75	0
Smith, C. Reginald, St.L.-L.A.#	.253	112	395	55	100	18	49	3
Speier, Chris, S.F.	.226	145	495	51	112	3	40	2

Player & Club	PCT	G	AB	R	H	HR	RBI	SB
Stargell, Wilver, Pitt.*	.257	117	428	54	110	20	65	2
Stennett, Renaldo, Pitt....	.257	157	654	59	168	2	60	18
Taveras, Franklin, Pitt. ...	.258	144	519	76	134	0	24	58
Trillo, J. Manuel, Chi.....	.238	158	582	42	139	4	59	17
Unser, Delbert, N.Y.-Mtl.*	.228	146	496	57	113	12	40	7
Watson, Robert, Hou.....	.313	157	585	76	183	16	102	3
Winfield, David, S.D.	.283	137	492	81	139	13	69	26
Wynn, James, Atl.	.207	148	449	75	93	17	66	16
Zisk, Richard, Pitt.	.289	155	581	91	168-	21	89	1

Individual Pitching

(140 or more innings pitched)

*Throws Lefthanded

Player & Club	ERA	W	L	G	IP	H	BB	SO
Andujar, Joaquin, Hou. .	3.61	9	10	28	172	163	75	59
Barr, James, S.F.	2.89	15	12	37	252	260	60	75
Billingham, John, Cin. ..	4.32	12	10	34	177	190	62	76
Bonham, William, Chi. ..	4.27	9	13	32	196	215	96	110
Burris, B. Ray, Chi.	3.11	15	13	37	249	251	70	112
Candelaria, John, Pitt.* .	3.15	16	7	32	220	173	60	138
Carlton, Steven, Phil.* ..	3.13	20	7	35	253	224	72	195
Carrithers, Donald, Mtl. .	4.44	6	12	34	140	153	78	71
Christenson, Larry, Phil.	3.67	13	8	32	169	199	42	54
Demery, Lawrence, Pitt. .	3.17	10	7	36	145	123	58	72
Denny, John, St.L.	2.52	11	9	30	207	189	74	74
Dierker, Lawrence, Hou.	3.69	13	14	28	188	171	72	112
Falcone, Peter, St. L.* ..	3.23	12	16	32	212	173	93	138
Forsch, Robert, St.L.	3.94	8	10	33	194	209	71	76
Friesleben, David, S.D. .	3.51	10	13	34	172	163	66	81
Fryman, Woodrow, Mtl.*	3.38	13	13	34	216	218	76	123
Halicki, Edward, S.F.	3.63	12	14	32	186	171	61	130
Hooton, Burt, L.A.	3.25	11	15	33	227	203	60	116
Hough, Charles, L.A. ...	2.20	12	8	77	143	102	77	81
John, Thomas, L.A.* ...	3.09	10	10	31	207	207	61	91
Jones, Randall, S.D.* ..	2.74	22	14	40	315	274	50	93
Kaat, James, Phil.*	3.47	12	14	38	228	241	32	83

Player and Club	ERA	W	L	G	IP	H	BB	SO
Kison, Bruce, Pitt.	3.08	14	9	31	193	180	52	98
Koosman, Jerry, N.Y.* .	2.70	21	10	34	247	205	66	200
Lolich, Michael, N.Y.* ..	3.22	8	13	31	193	184	52	120
Lonborg, James, Phil. ..	3.08	18	10	33	222	210	50	118
Matlack, Jonathan, N.Y.*	2.95	17	10	35	262	236	57	153
McGlothen, Lynn, St.L. .	3.91	13	15	33	205	209	68	106
Medich, George, Pitt. ...	3.52	8	11	29	179	193	48	86
Messersmith, John, Atl. .	3.04	11	11	29	207	166	74	135
Montefusco, John, S.F. .	2.85	16	14	37	253	224	74	172
Morton, Carl, Atl.	4.18	4	9	26	140	172	45	42
Niekro, Philip, Atl.	3.29	17	11	38	271	249	101	173
Nolan, Gary, Cin.	3.46	15	9	34	239	232	27	113
Norman, Fredie, Cin.* ..	3.10	12	7	33	180	153	70	126
Rasmussen, Harold, St.L.	3.54	6	12	43	150	139	54	76
Rau, Douglas, L.A.*	2.57	16	12	34	231	221	69	98
Renko, Steve, Mtl.-Chi. .	3.99	8	12	33	176	179	46	116
Reuschel, Ricky, Chi. ...	3.46	14	12	38	260	260	64	146
Reuss, Jerry, Pitt.*	3.53	14	9	31	209	209	51	108
Rhoden, Richard, L.A. ...	2.98	12	3	27	181	165	53	77
Richard, James, Hou. ...	2.75	20	15	39	291	221	151	214
Rogers, Stephen, Mtl. ...	3.21	7	17	33	230	212	69	150
Rooker, James, Pitt.* ...	3.35	15	8	30	199	201	72	92
Ruthven, Richard, Atl. ...	4.20	14	17	36	240	255	90	142
Seaver, G. Thomas, N.Y.	2.59	14	11	35	271	211	77	235
Stanhouse, Donald, Mtl.	3.77	9	12	34	184	182	92	79
Strom, Brent, S.D.*	3.28	12	16	36	211	188	73	103
Sutton, Donald, L.A. ...	3.06	21	10	35	268	231	82	161
Underwood, Thomas, Phil.*	3.52	10	5	33	156	154	63	94
Zachry, Patrick, Cin.....	2.74	14	7	38	204	170	83	143

American League

Individual Batting
(400 or more at-bats)

*Bats Lefthanded.   #Switch Hitter.

Player & Club	PCT	G	AB	R	H	HR	RBI	SB
Bando, Sal, Oak.	.240	158	550	75	132	27	84	20
Baylor, Don, Oak.	.247	157	595	85	147	15	68	52
Belanger, Mark, Balt.	.270	153	522	66	141	1	40	27
Bell, Buddy, Clev.	.281	159	604	75	170	7	60	3
Beniquez, Juan, Tex......	.255	145	478	49	122	0	33	17
Bochte, Bruce, Calif.*	.258	146	466	53	120	2	49	4
Bostock, Lyman, Minn.* ..	.323	128	474	75	153	4	60	12
Braun, Steve, Minn.*	.288	122	417	73	120	3	61	12
Brett, George, K.C.* ...:.	.333	159	645	94	215	7	67	21
Bumbry, Al, Balt.*	.251	133	450	71	113	9	36	42
Burleson, Rick, Bos.	.291	152	540	75	157	7	42	14
Burroughs, Jeff, Tex.	.237	158	604	71	143	18	86	0
Campaneris, Bert, Oak. ...	.256	149	536	67	137	1	52	54
Carew, Rod, Minn.*	.331	156	605	97	200	9	90	49
Carty, Rico, Clev.	.310	152	552	67	171	13	83	1
Chalk, Dave, Calf.	.217	142	438	39	95	0	33	0
Chambliss, Chris, N.Y.* ..	.293	156	641	79	188	17	96	1
Clines, Gene, Tex.	.276	116	446	52	123	0	38	11
Cooper, Cecil, Bos.*	.282	123	451	66	127	15	78	7
Cowens, Al, K.C.	.265	152	581	71	154	3	59	23
DeCinces, Doug, Balt.....	.234	129	440	36	103	11	42	8
Dent, Bucky, Chgo.......	.246	158	562	44	138	2	52	3
Doyle, Denny, Bos.*	.250	117	432	51	108	0	26	8
Evans, Dwight, Bos.	.242	146	501	61	121	17	62	6
Fisk, Carlton, Bos.	.255	134	487	76	124	17	58	12
Ford, Dan, Minn.........	.267	145	514	87	137	20	86	17
Garner, Phil, Oak.	.261	159	555	54	145	8	74	35
Garr, Ralph, Chgo.*	.300	136	527	63	158	4	36	14
Grich, Bobby, Balt.	.266	144	518	93	138	13	54	14
Grieve, Tom, Tex.	.255	149	546	57	139	20	81	4
Hargrove, Mike, Tex.*	.287	151	541	80	155	7	58	2
Harrah, Toby, Tex.	.260	155	584	64	152	15	67	8

Player & Club	PCT	G	AB	R	H	HR	RBI	SB
Hendrick, George, Clev. ...	.265	149	551	72	146	25	81	4
Hisle, Larry, Minn.	.272	155	581	81	158	14	96	31
Horton, Willie, Det.	.262	114	401	40	105	14	56	0
Howell, Roy, Tex.*	.253	140	491	55	124	8	53	1
Jackson, Reggie, Balt.* ...	.277	134	498	84	138	27	91	28
Jackson, Ron, Calf.......	.227	127	410	44	93	8	40	5
Johnson, Alex, Det.	.268	125	429	41	115	6	45	14
Joshua, Von, Milw.*	.267	107	423	44	113	5	28	8
Kuiper, Duane, Clev.*	.263	135	506	47	133	0	37	10
Leflore, Ron, Det. ....:	.316	135	544	93	172	4	39	58
Lemon, Chet, Chgo.	.246	132	451	46	111	4	38	13
Lezcano, Sixto, Milw.	.285	145	513	53	146	7	56	14
Lynn, Fred, Bos.*	.314	132	507	76	159	10	65	14
Manning, Rick, Clev.*	.292	138	552	73	161	6	43	16
May, Lee, Balt.	.258	148	530	61	137	25	109	4
Mayberry, John, K.C.* ...	.232	161	594	76	138	13	95	3
McRae, Hal, K.C.	.332	149	527	75	175	8	73	22
Money, Don, Milw.	.267	117	439	51	117	12	62	6
Munson, Thurman, N.Y. ...	.302	152	616	79	186	17	105	14
Nettles, Graig, N.Y.*	.254	158	583	88	148	32	93	11
North, Bill, Oak.#	.276	154	590	91	163	2	31	75
Orta, Jorge, Chgo.*	.274	158	636	74	174	14	72	24
Otis, Amos, K.C.........	.279	153	592	93	165	18	86	26
Patek, Fred, K.C.........	.241	144	432	58	104	1	43	51
Randall, Bob, Minn.	.267	153	475	55	127	1	34	3
Randle, Lenny, Tex.#	.224	142	539	53	121	1	51	30
Randolph, Willie, N.Y.	.267	125	430	59	115	1	40	37
Remy, Jerry, Calf.*	.263	143	502	64	132	0	28	35
Rice, Jim, Bos.	.282	153	581	75	164	25	85	8
Rivers, Mickey, N.Y.*	.312	137	590	95	184	8	67	43
Rodriguez, Aurelio, Det. ...	.240	128	480	40	115	8	50	0
Rudi, Joe, Oak.	.270	130	500	54	135	13	94	6
Scott, George, Milw......	.274	156	606	73	166	18	77	0
Singleton, Ken, Balt.# ...	.278	154	544	62	151	13	70	2
Smalley, Roy, Minn.-Tex.#	.259	144	513	61	133	3	44	2
Spencer, Jim, Chgo.	.253	150	518	53	131	14	70	6
Staub, Rusty, Det.*	.299	161	589	73	176	15	96	3
Sundberg, Jim, Tex.	.228	140	448	33	102	3	34	0
Tenace, Gene, Oak.......	.249	128	417	64	104	22	66	5

Player & Club	PCT	G	AB	R	H	HR	RBI	SB
Thompson, Jason, Det.*	.218	123	412	45	90	17	54	2
Washington, Claudell, Oak.*	.257	134	490	65	126	5	53	37
White, Frank, K.C.	.229	152	446	39	102	2	46	20
White, Roy, N.Y.#	.286	156	626	104	179	14	65	31
Wynegar, Butch, Minn.# .	.260	149	534	58	139	10	69	0
Yastrzemski, Carl, Bos.* ..	.267	155	546	71	146	21	102	5
Yount, Robin, Milw.	.252	161	638	59	161	2	54	16

Individual Pitching

(120 or more innings pitched)

*Pitches Lefthanded.

Player and Club	ERA	W	L	G	IP	H	BB	SO
Alexander, Doyle, N.Y.-Balt.	3.36	13	9	30	201	172	63	58
Augustine, Jerry, Milw.*	3.30	9	12	39	172	167	56	59
Bahnsen, Stan, Oak.....	3.34	8	7	35	143	124	43	82
Bare, Ray, Det.	4.63	7	8	30	134	157	51	59
Barrios, Francisco, Chgo.	4.31	5	9	35	142	136	46	81
Bibby, Jim, Clev.	3.20	13	7	34	163	162	56	84
Bird, Doug, K.C.	3.36	12	10	39	198	191	31	107
Blue, Vida, Oak.*	2.35	18	13	37	298	268	63	166
Blyleven, Bert, Tex.-Minn.	2.87	13	16	36	298	283	81	219
Brett, Ken, Chi.-N.Y.* ..	3.28	10	12	29	203	173	76	92
Briles, Nelson. Tex. ...	3.26	11	9	32	210	224	47	98
Brown, Jackie, Clev.....	4.25	9	1	32	180	193	55	104
Campbell, Bill, Minn. ...	3.00	17	5	78	168	145	62	115
Cleveland, Reggie, Bos. .	3.07	10	9	41	170	159	61	76
Colborn, Jim, Milw.	3.70	9	15	32	226	232	54	101
Dobson, Pat, Clev.	3.48	16	12	35	217	226	65	117
Eckersley, Dennis, Clev..	3.44	13	12	36	199	155	78	200
Ellis, Dock, N.Y.	3.18	17	8	32	212	195	76	65
Fidrych, Mark, Det.	2.34	19	9	31	250	217	53	97
Figueroa, Ed, N.Y.	3.01	19	10	34	257	237	94	119
Fitzmorris, Al, K.C.	3.07	15	11	35	220	227	56	80
Garland, Wayne, Balt. ..	2.68	20	7	38	232	224	64	113

Player and Club	ERA	W	L	G	IP	H	BB	SO
Goltz, Dave, Minn.	3.36	14	14	36	249	239	91	133
Gossage, Rich, Chgo. . .	3.94	9	17	31	224	214	90	135
Grimsley, Ross, Balt.* . .	3.94	8	7	28	137	143	35	41
Hargan, Steve, Tex.	3.63	8	8	35	124	127	38	63
Hartzell, Paul, Calf.	2.77	7	4	37	166	166	43	51
Hassler, Andy, K.C.-Cal.*	3.61	5	12	33	147	139	56	61
Hiller, John, Det.*	2.38	12	8	56	121	93	67	117
Holtzman, Ken, N.Y.-Balt.*	3.64	14	11	34	247	265	70	66
Hughes, Jim, Minn.	4.98	9	14	37	177	190	73	87
Hunter, Catfish, N.Y. . . .	3.52	17	15	36	299	268	68	173
Jenkins, Ferguson, Bos. .	3.27	12	11	30	209	201	43	142
Johnson, Bart, Chgo. . . .	4.73	9	16	32	211	231	62	91
Kirkwood, Don, Calf. . . .	4.61	6	12	28	158	167	57	78
Leonard, Dennis, K.C. . .	3.51	17	10	35	259	247	70	150
May, Rudy, Balt.-N.Y.* .	3.72	15	10	35	220	205	70	109
Monge, Sid, Calf.*	3.36	6	7	32	118	108	49	53
Palmer, Jim, Balt.	2.51	22	13	40	315	255	84	159
Pattin, Marty, K.C.	2.49	8	14	44	141	114	38	65
Perry, Gaylord, Tex.	3.24	15	14	32	250	232	52	143
Pole, Dick, Bos.	4.31	6	5	31	121	131	48	49
Roberts, Dave, Det.* . . .	4.00	16	17	36	252	254	63	79
Rodriguez, Eduardo, Milw.	3.64	5	13	45	136	124	65	77
Ross, Gary, Calf.	3.00	8	16	34	225	224	58	100
Ruhle, Vern, Det.	3.92	9	12	32	200	227	59	88
Ryan, Nolan, Calf.	3.36	17	18	39	284	193	183	327
Singer, Bill, Minh.-Tex. .	3.68	13	10	36	237	233	96	97
Slaton, Jim, Milw.	3.44	14	15	38	293	287	94	138
Splittorff, Paul, K.C.* . . .	3.96	11	8	26	159	169	59	59
Tanana, Frank, Calf.* . . .	2.44	19	10	34	288	212	73	261
Tiant, Luis, Bos.	3.06	21	12	38	279	274	64	131
Torrez, Mike, Oak.	2.50	16	12	39	266	231	87	115
Travers, Bill, Milw.*	2.81	15	16	34	240	211	95	120
Umbarger, Jim, Tex.* . .	3.15	10	12	30	197	208	54	105
Waits, Rick, Clev.*	3.99	7	9	26	124	143	54	65
Wise, Rick, Bos.	3.54	14	11	34	224	218	48	93

HOW THEY'LL FINISH IN '77

National League East
1. Philadelphia Phils
2. Pittsburgh Pirates
3. New York Mets
4. St. Louis Cardinals
5. Montreal Expos
6. Chicago Cubs

National League West
1. Cincinnati Reds
2. Los Angeles Dodgers
3. San Diego Padres
4. Atlanta Braves
5. Houston Astros
6. San Francisco Giants

American League East
1. New York Yankees
2. Boston Red Sox
3. Cleveland Indians
4. Detroit Tigers
5. Baltimore Orioles
6. Milwaukee Brewers
7. Toronto Blue Jays

American League West
1. California Angels
2. Kansas City Royals
3. Texas Rangers
4. Minnesota Twins
5. Chicago White Sox
6. Oakland A's
7. Seattle Mariners

American League Champs: New York Yankees
National League Champs: Cincinnati Reds
World Champs: Cincinnati

LATE NEWS

The Los Angeles Dodgers traded outfielder BILL BUCKNER and infielder IVAN De-JESUS to the Chicago Cubs for outfielder RICK MONDAY and pitcher MIKE GARMAN. The Dodgers also sent infielder TED SIZEMORE to Philadelphia for catcher JOHNNY OATES.

The Atlanta Braves purchased pitcher STEVE KLINE from Toledo. Commissioner Bowie Kuhn suspended Braves' owner TED TURNER for tampering with ex-Giant out-fielder GARY MATTHEWS.

The Toronto Blue Jays signed pitcher LLOYD ALLEN and second baseman PEDRO GARCIA.

Houston dealt catcher SKIP JUTZE to Seattle for ALAN GRIFFIN.

Milwaukee signed relief pitcher KEN SAUNDERS. He replaces DANNY FRISELLA who was killed in a dune-buggy accident.

Two other major leaguers also died: California shortstop MIKE MILEY in an auto accident, and Texas infielder DANNY THOMPSON of leukemia.

The Chicago White Sox received LARRY ANDERSON from Toronto, completing the deal that gave the Blue Jays catcher PHIL ROOF.